PASSPORT
BRAZIL

Passport To The World

Passport Argentina
Passport China
Passport France
Passport Germany
Passport Hong Kong
Passport India
Passport Indonesia
Passport Israel
Passport Italy
Passport Japan
Passport Korea
Passport Malaysia
Passport Mexico
Passport Poland
Passport Russia
Passport Singapore
Passport South Africa
Passport Spain
Passport Taiwan
Passport Thailand
Passport United Kingdom
Passport USA
Passport Vietnam

PASSPORT BRAZIL

Your Pocket Guide to Brazilian Business, Customs & Etiquette

Elizabeth Herrington

Passport Series Editor: Barbara Szerlip

WORLD TRADE PRESS®
Professional Books for International Trade

World Trade Press
1505 Fifth Avenue
San Rafael, California 94901 USA
Tel: (415) 454-9934
Fax: (415) 453-7980
USA Orderline: (800) 833-8586
E-mail: WorldPress@aol.com
http://www.worldtradepress.com

"Passport to the World" concept: Edward G. Hinkelman
Cover design: Peter Jones, Marge Wilhite
Book design and layout: Joe Reif
Illustrations: Tom Watson

Passport BRAZIL
Copyright © 1998 by World Trade Press. All Rights Reserved.

Reproduction of any part of this work beyond that permitted by the United States Copyright Act without the express written permission of the copyright holder is unlawful. Requests for permission or further information should be addressed to World Trade Press at the address above.

This publication is designed to provide general information concerning the cultural aspects of doing business with people from a particular country. It is sold with the understanding that the publisher is not engaged in rendering legal or any other professional services. If legal advice or other expert assistance is required, the services of a competent professional person should be sought.

Library of Congress Cataloging-in-Publication Data
Herrington, Elizabeth.
Passport Brazil: your pocket guide to Brazilian business, customs & etiquette / Elizabeth Herrington.
p. cm. -- (Passport to the world)
Includes bibliographical references (p.)
ISBN 1-885073-18-6
1. Corporate culture -- Brazil. 2. Business etiquette -- Brazil. 3. Industrial management -- Social aspects -- Brazil. 4. Negotiation in Business -- Brazil. 5. Intercultural communication. I. Title. II. Series.
HD58.7.H465 1997
390'.00981 -- dc21
97-26551 CIP

Printed in the United States of America

Table of Contents
BRAZIL

The Awakening Giant

Overview

- Brazil Quick Look 6
- 1: Country Facts 7
- 2: The Brazilians 11
- 3: Cultural Stereotypes 28
- 4: Regional Differences 34

Business Environment

- 5: Government & Business 39
- 6: The Work Environment 46
- 7: Women in Business 51
- 8: Making Connections 55
- 9: Strategies for Success 57
- 10: Time 60
- 11: Business Meetings 62
- 12: Negotiating with Brazilians 66
- 13: Business Outside the Law 70

Customs & Etiquette

- 14: Names & Greetings 74
- 15: Communication Styles 76
- 16: Customs 78
- 17: Dress & Appearance 81
- 18: Entertaining 83
- 19: Socializing 86

Additional Information

- 20: Basic Brazilian Portuguese 90
- 21: Correspondence 91
- 22: Useful Telephone Numbers 92
- 23: Books & Internet Addresses 93

BRAZIL
Quick Look

Official name   Federative Republic of Brazil
Land area   3,286,470 sq mi
       (8,511,965 sq km)
Capital   Brasília
Largest city   São Paulo
Highest elevation   Pico da Neblina
       9,888 ft (3,014 m)

People
    Population   160 million
    Density   17.6 per sq km
    Official language Portuguese
    Major religions   Catholic (70%), Protestant, Jewish, Afro-Brazilian

Economy (1995)
    GDP   US$563 billion
    Per capita   US$4,608
    Foreign trade (1996)
       Imports   US $53.3 billion
       Exports   US$47.8 billion
    Deficit   US$5.5 billion
    Principal trade partners
       U.S., E.C., Middle East
       Latin America, Japan
    Currency   1 real (R$) = 100 centavos
    Exchange rate   R$1 = US$1 (9/97)

Education and health
    Literacy (1992)   80%
    Universities   851 institutes of higher learning
    Hospital beds   3.2 beds per 1,000 people
    Physicians (1992) 200,000
    Life expectancy (1995) Women – 67 years
       Men – 57 years

BRAZIL

1 Country Facts

Geography and Demographics

The largest country in South America, Brazil borders the Atlantic Ocean and shares common boundaries with every country on the continent except Chile and Ecuador. It's also the fifth-largest country in the world, after the Russian Federation, Canada, China and the U.S. Its terrain varies from the rich farmland of the south to the savannalike areas and tropical rainforest of the north.

Except for a handful of islands, Brazil is a single land mass, organized into 26 states and the federal district. The equator passes through the north of the country near Macapá. Brazil's greatest width, 2,684 miles (4,319 kilometers), is almost the same as its greatest distance from north to south, 2,731 miles (4,395 km.).

The Amazon, most of which lies within the country's borders, is the world's largest rainforest. Brazil's fluvial system, which boasts eight drainage basins, is one of the world's most extensive. The Amazon River is the world's largest in terms of volume and the second longest (after the Nile) — 4,087 miles (6577 km.) long. Of that total, 2,246 miles (3,615 km.) are within Brazil's boundaries. The Amazon River basin contains one-fifth of the world's fresh water.

Brazilians are mainly of Portuguese and African descent, although, much like the U.S., Brazil is a nation of immigrants, and there are also huge communities of European, Middle Eastern and Asian descendants. Caucasians make up about half the country's population. The Indian population, nearly decimated forty years ago (see "The Yanomami and Other Indigenous Peoples," page 21), is now growing. Brazil's official religion is Catholicism; however, many world religions, including Afro-Brazilian cults, are represented.

Climate

Brazil's climate is mostly tropical, but eases into subtropical and temperate as you go farther south. The Tropic of Capricorn cuts right through São Paulo, separating the sub-tropical from the temperate zone.

In the north, the temperature remains fairly steady all year round, hovering at 90°F (32°C), while in the southeast regions of Rio de Janeiro and São Paulo, it gets that hot in the summer (December-February). In the winter, temperatures can decline to around 55°F (13°C) in Rio and 45°F (7°C) in São Paulo, though not for more than a week or two.

In the south, temperatures have been known to dip below freezing, but that's rare. It even snows occasionally in Brazil — in a mountainous region called São Joaquim in the southern state of Santa Catarina. When that happens, maybe once per season, it's a major event and the top story on a slow news day.

Business Hours

Office hours are typically 9 A.M. to 6 P.M., with a 90-minute lunch break. In most big cities, banks are open from 10 A.M. to 4:30 P.M. and closed on weekends. Automatic Teller Machines are readily available in most locations.

The big department stores and malls are usually open from 9 A.M. to 10 P.M. and close on Sundays. Smaller retail establishments close Saturday at noon and remain closed until Monday. Pharmacies have an arrangement whereby one in every four in a given location remains open on Sunday or a holiday, and the other three post the address of the open pharmacy on their shuttered doors.

National Holidays

New Year's Day . . . . January 1
> New Year's Eve is celebrated with fireworks and balls. Devotees of the Afro-Brazilian cult *candomble* send out little paper ships lit by candles in honor of the goddess of the sea, Yemanja.

Shrove Tuesday (Carnival) . . . . . 41 days before Easter
> A.k.a. Terça-feira gorda, this is the last day that Catholics can eat meat or celebrate before Ash Wednesday. The Monday before is considered an unofficial holiday.

Good Friday . . . . varies
Easter. . . . . varies
Tiradentes Day. . . . . April 21
> Commemorates the death of 19th-century freedom fighter Tiradentes.

Labor Day. . . . . May 1
Corpus Christi . . . . June 6
> A feast that honors the Eucharist.

Independence Day . . . . September 7
> On this day in 1822, Dom Pedro declared independence from Portugal (though it remained a monarchy for 67 more years).

Patron Saint of Brazil Day..... October 12
   Millions make a pilgrimage to see the image of Nossa Senhora de Aparecida.

All Souls' Day............... November 2
   In memory of deceased loved ones, Brazil's cemeteries are packed with visitors all day.

Proclamation of the Republic .. November 15
   On this date in 1889, the military ousted Brazil's last monarch — Dom Pedro I — and proclaimed the Republic of Brazil.

Christmas................. December 25
   Celebrated with family dinners, attendance at Midnight Mass, a visit by *Papai Noel*, and the exchanging of gifts.

The Brazilians

Paradoxical Nation

Brazil has often been described as a land of contrasts and paradoxes. Because its huge landmass spans both equatorial and temperate zones, many regions enjoy two annual harvests that could, in theory, feed much of the rest of the world, as well as its own people. Yet crop failures are frequent, and hunger-related illness are common.

The country is blessed with huge natural resources — gems, gold, enormous forests, and waterfalls that, as Eleanor Roosevelt once said, "make Niagara look like a dentist's faucet." And Brazil boasts the world's 8th-largest economy. Between 1900 and 1970, only Japan registered higher economic growth. Yet ignorance of the most basic facts of childcare condemns vast numbers of children to early deaths. Only a third of the population is served by a sewerage system, 30 percent are without piped water, and the majority live in poverty.

It's a melting pot of Native Americans, African-Americans and Europeans, and a considerable amount of intermarriage has created an extraordinary spectrum of skin color. Still, light skin reigns. Nearly 40 percent of non-whites have had four years or less of schooling. The black illiteracy rate is twice that of whites; when it comes to salaries, the reverse equation applies. (The legal minimum wage is US$112 a month.)

Many outsiders harbor a romantic view of Brazil as a land of music, soccer, sex and swaying coconut palms, and while those images apply, it's also true that the country is home to breathtaking urban squalor and violence.

The police, too, are sometimes violent (and often go unpunished), but they're just as often ineffectual against such well-organized groups as the drug gangs that rule Rio's *favelas* (shanty-town slums). Well-meaning government human rights policies, in turn, are sometimes overridden in the fight against drug trafficking.

Brazil's societal paradoxes are most evident during Carnival. Once a year the poorest of the poor — members of the *escolas de samba* (samba schools) that compete for awards in the four nightly parades during these pre-Lenten festivities — dress up in costumes rivaling Las Vegas chorus lines and, for four days, they're on the top of the world. The rest of the year, they live from hand to mouth and dream of next year's Carnival.

Yet through a mixture of compromise and a pervasive "live and let live" attitude, Brazilians have avoided the clashes that such inequities bring about in other cultures. Negotiation leads to solution and has led Brazil to overcome huge economic and societal setbacks that would keep many other developing countries firmly entrenched in the Third World.

Colonial Chess

Discovered by Portuguese navigator Pedro Alvarez Cabral in 1500, Brazil was colonized in 1533. In 1549, under Portuguese King João III, Salvador became Brazil's first capital, and it remained so for 214 years.

The colonial government began to encourage Portugal's citizenry to emigrate. The new settlers were mostly colonial governors, Jesuit priests, and adventure-seekers of dubious merit. The former were expected to develop the land at their own expense and to trade exclusively with Portugal. Because the Jesuits managed to educate the Indians and to protect them from forced labor (mostly on sugar plantations and tobacco farms), the colonists soon resorted to importing West Africans as slaves — some four million of them, more than any other country in the Western Hemisphere. Miscegenation was encouraged by the Portuguese crown as a means of populating the colony.

Battles with the French during the 16th century were common. The Portuguese finally drove the French out of the Rio de Janeiro region in 1565. For the next 65 years, Portuguese sovereignty remained unchallenged. Then, in 1630, the Dutch West Indian Company seized control of key sugar-cane plantations in the northeastern state of Pernambuco. Twenty-four years later, the Dutch were driven out by the combined efforts of the colonists and the Portuguese army.

Toward the end of the 17th century, gold was discovered in the southeastern state of Minas Gerais, and thousands of new settlers flooded in in search of easy riches. In response, the Portuguese crown began demanding taxes in the form of gold.

In 1789, after Portugal increased its gold tax, an independence movement arose, but it proved unsuccessful. Brazil was to live under a monarchy for the next 100 years.

In 1807, the royal family was forced into Brazilian exile after Napoleon conquered Portugal. King João VI ruled the mother country from its colony until he and his family were able to return home in 1821. When João's son Dom Pedro I became regent, he declared independence from Portugal, creating the Brazilian Empire.

From Monarchy to Military Rule

Pedro, a hugely unpopular monarch who clung to his royal privilege despite growing liberal tendencies among his subjects, abdicated in 1831. His 5-year-old son Pedro II became Prince Regent, and then in 1840, at the tender age of 15, emperor. Pedro II spent much of his reign engaged in border wars, notably a war with Paraguay (1865-1870) that Brazil won, aided by Argentina and Uruguay, but at the cost of heavy human losses.

The war set the stage for the military to come to power. In 1888, when, under much pressure from abolitionists and trading partners, notably the U.S., Emperor Dom Pedro II finally declared slavery illegal (a quarter century after Abraham Lincoln's Emancipation Proclamation went into effect), disgruntled wealthy landowners joined forces with the military and ousted him. (The story goes that, tripping at a fancy dress ball just weeks before he was deposed, Dom Pedro II joked, "The empire stumbled, but it has not yet fallen!") For the next hundred years, until Brazil's sixth constitution was drafted in 1988, the military would be the single-most-powerful institution in the country.

The Getulio Vargas Years

A contemporary of Italy's Mussolini, Spain's Franco and Argentina's Peron, Getulio Vargas was installed as president by a military coup in 1930 and stayed at the center of power for the next 25 years. Vargas liked to portray himself as the father of the poor, and schoolbooks showed his photograph superimposed over the image of a large group of children — smiling down like a benevolent god.

Like Peron, Vargas used Brazil's shift from an agricultural society to an industrialized one as his main political focus, concentrating his appeal on the urban working masses. He legalized labor unions, but made them subject to federal government control. In 1937, he threw out the constitution and gave himself dictatorial powers — the only way, he insisted, to save the country from Communism. He joined the Allies in World War II, making Brazil the only Latin American country to send troops to the front.

Although ousted from office in 1945 by military forces (who thought he was starting to move uncomfortably far to the Left), Vargas remained an influential advisor and managed to get himself re-elected in the 1950 "indirect" elections (i.e., the vote was left to Congressional party leaders) and to reign for another four years. In August 1954, the military once again rattled its sabers, offering him the choice of either resigning or being overthrown. Vargas did neither, choosing instead to commit suicide.

From Ditadura to Democracy

In 1955, Juscelino Kubitschek was elected president. A visionary leader, he transferred the national's capital from Rio de Janeiro to Brasília, the country's geographic center, in 1960.

Designed by world-renowned architect Oscar Niemeyer and landscape artist Burle Marx, Brasília was a noble but impractical idea — a mass of freeways and viaducts, with no parks, no beach, and little in the way of diversion, and no way to get around without a car. This was the 1950s, when petroleum was expected to last forever. Brazil had just begun drilling its own oil, in the hope of being self-sufficient by the year 2000.

(Today, Brasília is surrounded by so-called satellite towns where those who built the city live in poverty with their families; there's little work for them, but they don't wish to return to their former, even poorer towns. Brazilians joke that the best thing about Brasília are its hourly flights to Rio and São Paulo.)

Kubitschek was succeeded by leftist President João Goulart, whose CIA-sponsored overthrow in 1964 led to 21 years of uninterrupted military regime (known as the *ditadura*), during which five army generals held presidential office. Using the excuse of "mounting subversive activities," the infamous decree of December 13, 1968 was issued, suspending all civil liberties, and in its wake came a relentless war against Brazil's popular arts. For the next two decades, repression, false arrests, rape, murder and torture were the norm. In the latter case, Brazilians lent their humor to the creation of colorful nicknames. A "Chinese bath" referred to being held under water for long periods of time. *Pau de arara* (parrot's perch) was a way of hanging someone upside down. And "Christ the Redeemer"(named after Rio's famous statue) was used to describe the torture of being made to stand holding telephone books with outstretched arms for days on end.

During the so-called Brazilian Miracle of the 1970s, the booming economy distracted Brazilians from the restrictive military regime. But in the 1980s, when the Latin American debt crisis soared out of control and Brazil began suffering astronomical inflation rates and a deepening recession, opposition to the military increased, both from citizens and foreign governments. Little by little, controls were loosened and Brazil began inching its way toward democracy.

Today, Brazil is teetering on the threshold of the First World. Its democratically elected administration has resolved the debt crisis, brought inflation down to tolerable levels, and is overseeing excellent economic growth. The country still suffers huge social problems, but the government's emphasis on health, education, privatization and free trade, among other progressive issues, should steer Brazil away from its former emphasis on the future and toward more attention to the immediate needs of the present.

Language

Nearly 200 million people speak Portuguese, making it the eighth most widely spoken language in the world. Of that total, 154 million are Brazilians and 11 million are Portuguese, with inhabitants of former colonies in Africa and Asia making up the balance.

While Portuguese reads like Spanish, its pronunciation is very nasal and it can take years to master. Its grammar is so complex and archaic that even many Brazilians have a poor grasp of it. As a result, there's often a huge difference between what's written and what's spoken.

Brazilians speak the language of their colonial founders with a twist. Brazilian Portuguese is to the language of Portugal as American English is to its British mother tongue. The two forms are mutually intelligible, but Brazilian Portuguese is peppered with such indigenous tribal words as *capim* (grass), *jacaré* (alligator), and the name of the coastal resort city *Ubatuba* (land of many boats), among others. Contributions from slaves imported from Africa include *dendê* (palm oil), *samba* (perhaps Brazil's most famous musical style) and *Axé* (a greeting meaning, roughly, all good things to you.)

With the advent of 20th century technology, the gap between the European and American forms of the language widened, as each country had its own way of borrowing or creating words to describe new inventions. Thus, "bus" in Portugal is *autocarro*, while in Brazil it's *onibus*.

Portuguese is pronounced somewhat like Spanish, but with a nasality akin to French. During the 19th century, it was influenced by Europeans (other than the Portuguese) who immigrated to the central and southern parts of the country — Italians, in particular. *Ciao* is a much more common form of "good-bye" than the Portuguese *adeus* in most parts of the country.

Brazilian Portuguese varies greatly from region to region. The São Paulo dialect, heavily influenced by the vast Italian community, is seen by other Brazilians as harsh, while the language spoken in Rio de Janeiro, just 400 kilometers away, is softer and more sibilant, with the "s" sound usually pronounced as "sh." In Rio Grande do Sul, where the *gaúchos* (cowboys) live, the language is a little closer to Spanish. Indeed, in many towns on the Argentine and Paraguayan borders to the south, the patois is a mix of the two languages.

Friendly and Easy-going

Brazilians are, for the most part, ready with a smile or a witty comment on the latest headlines. It's very easy to make friends here, although such casual friendships can often be superficial. It's common for a Brazilian to invite you over to his house (*passe lá em casa*), but don't just drop in unless you're absolutely sure of the invitation.

People are eager to please and reticent to say "no." Instead, you'll be given the impression that the matter is under consideration. If you say, for example, "Let's have lunch next Saturday," it's the rare Brazilian who will consult his appointment book and set up a time. Instead, he'll just say yes, even if he has something else in mind.

Brazilians are very tolerant people. For example, homosexuals, if not universally accepted, are viewed more as objects of curiosity than as pariahs. Most homosexual movie stars and professional singers in Brazil are quite open about their preferences.

Family, Brazilian-style

Family values are alive and well in Brazil, although the definition of family is often somewhat looser than it is in other countries.

Brazil has the largest Catholic population of any country in the world. Divorce only became legal in 1977, and even now it remains a difficult and drawn-out procedure. Instead, many Brazilians obtain a legal separation and set up housekeeping with a second spouse in a common-law marriage, the offspring of which are considered legitimate. Meanwhile, fundamentalist Protestant sects are growing in popularity, bringing a conservative message and the hope of earthly rewards in return for tithes — in sharp contrast to Catholic tenets.

Another informal interpretation of "family" is the phenomenon of adopted children, who aren't adopted in the strict legal sense. Many families, especially in smaller, poorer regions, will accept a child from a mother who can't afford to keep it —

often raising the child as a servant or farm helper. The child becomes a de facto member of the family.

Many men have mistresses; some are discreet, others are quite open about it. In cities like São Paulo, there are entire apartment buildings known as *rendezvous*, their one-room studios reserved for illicit trysts.

In the cities, two-income nuclear families are becoming quite common. But with labor so cheap, parents can afford household help in the form of maids or nannies.

Orixás

Syncretism, the fusion of two religious beliefs, plays a strong role in Brazilian society. Often, when a Brazilian is asked his religion, he'll say, "Oh, I'm Catholic, but I do pay homage to my *Orixá*."

Orixás (personal saints) are part of Candomblé, the belief system that accompanied enslaved, Brazil-bound West Africans, particularly those of the Yoruba/Sudanese tribe. Forced into Catholicism by their masters, the slaves translated their *Orixás* to Catholic saints. For example, Yemanjá (the deity of the sea) is often fused with the Virgin Mary and Ogum (the deity of war) with St. George.

The ceremonies of Candomblé are very beautiful and mystical, akin to Caribbean voodoo in its origins and some of its practices. It's especially prevalent in Bahia, but offerings of flower, food and candles to the *Orixás* can be found at crossroads or near churches throughout the country, in both big cities and small towns.

Although referred to as an Afro-Brazilian cult, it has followers of every stripe. Descendants of the Japanese worship at Candomblé houses in São Paulo, while Brazilians of Italian origin gather for similar worship in the South.

The Yanomami & Other Indigenous Peoples

Until the Portuguese arrived in 1500, Brazil was a haven for numerous indigenous tribes — tribes that proved vulnerable to such unknown European diseases as influenza and smallpox. Many who didn't succumb were at the mercy of bounty hunters and *bandeirantes* (adventurers), murdered en masse by rubber barons (who wanted their land and their servitude), or forced to flee by miners (who slashed trees and burned vast swaths of land in their ruthless quest for gold). Between 1900 and 1967, ninety-eight indigenous tribes were annihilated. It wasn't until 1990, after sixteen Yanomami Indians were murdered, that the government officially banned miners from the Amazon Basin and ordered the destruction of more than 100 Amazonian landing strips.

During the last four decades, the Indian population has made a comeback. According to government data, it now numbers about 260,000, is roughly organized into 200 groups, and speaks 180 different languages. An additional five million Brazilians who can claim Indian ancestry live as fully integrated citizens, virtually indistinguishable from the rest of Brazilian society.

Brazil's 1988 Constitution expanded previous provisions for the protection of indigenous groups and the preservation of their traditional community life, and it recognized, for the first time, the rights of these groups to all lands they've "traditionally" occupied — including productive terrain, travel areas and sacred sites, not merely, as in the past, areas in the immediate vicinity of inhabited villages. Although all Indian lands are still recognized as federal lands, the permanent and exclusive right to use them now rests in tribal hands; mining and developing hydroelectric potential are permitted only when explicitly authorized by Congress.

The federal government continues to develop and implement a wide range of protections for self-sustained community life, autonomous organization of Indian communities, and the preservation of languages and traditions. Access to health care and education is a priority, with special emphasis given to bilingual teaching methods. The full participation of Indian communities in the decision-making process on matters of concern to them is encouraged.

This nationwide program is complemented by a special initiative that provides emergency assistance to the Yanomami, Brazil's best known and most recently "discovered" Indian group and perhaps the last Neolithic-age community in the world. Living scattered along the Brazilian-Venezuelan border, the Yanomami total 25,000 individuals, 10,000 of whom reside within Brazil's borders. They remained virtually isolated — hunting, fishing and gathering bananas in the rainforest, preserving their history orally through chants, and believing in animal and plant spirits and the healing power of shamans — until a gold rush in the late 1970s brought in a flood of outsiders. A worldwide campaign to protect Yanomami lands resulted in the demarcation, in 1991, of a contiguous Yanomami reservation of 36,000 square miles (twice the size of Belgium).

The Cachet of Coffee

The first national crop was sugar, which supported the Portuguese crown. Then came rubber, but the trees only grew wild and in malarial jungles, defying cultivation. Still, with the help of forced labor, Brazil's rubber barons became so wealthy that they built an opera house in the middle of the jungle and sent their laundry to Paris. Rubber reigned until 1876, when an enterprising

Englishman, posing as an orchid hunter, smuggled a few hundred rubber tree seeds out and on to Indonesia, where, within thirty years, the thriving trees were producing latex. Then came coffee, which also gave birth to numerous side industries — its carbohydrates used in the manufacture of plastics and dyestuffs, its proteins to modify certain tars and oils. The city of São Paulo was built with coffee revenues.

In the 1930s, there was so much coffee in Brazil — Frank Sinatra even sang a song about it — that exporters actually dumped coffee beans into the sea in an attempt to rally prices. Today, while Brazil is still the world's top producer (with Colombia running a close second), the commodity no longer figures as importantly in the national revenue.

Once Brazil's top export commodity, coffee today represents just 1 percent of export revenue. Vulnerability to frost — Brazil is the only coffee producer in the world subject to frost and whole plantations have been wiped out — has caused some coffee growers to move north to warmer climes. Others have turned to more lucrative, lower-maintenance crops like sugar cane and soybeans.

São Paulo was Brazil's first big coffee state, as planters gradually switched from cotton to coffee in the mid-19th century. Coffee had become quite a fashionable beverage in Europe and the planters realized they'd hit upon a niche with little competition. The state soon began to recruit immigrants to help with the planting and harvest.

Nowadays, the market has shifted to countries like Colombia, Kenya and Jamaica, and local producers lament the loss of status to their competitors. Still, "coffee culture" continues to shape the lives of people in small towns in the states of Parana, São Paulo and, especially, Minas Gerais, towns that were built with coffee money. Growers, along with those involved in the allied industries, have an emotional attachment to the crop unequaled by any other aspect of Brazilian farming.

How Brazilians See Themselves

Brazilians believe themselves to be blessed by God — *Deus é Brasileiro* (God is a Brazilian), they say — with good weather, fertile soil, great musicality and sportsmanship. They believe that their women are the most beautiful in the world and their musicians the best. Yet sometimes a Brazilian will sit back, shake his head, and wonder why, with all that good fortune, Brazil still can't quite get its act together — the welfare and pension systems are teetering on bankruptcy, the civil service needs to be overhauled, agrarian reform is long overdue (1 percent of the farms have half the usable land), and decent public school education has yet to be made available to all.

Brazilians are sensitive to what they consider the dangers of "cultural imperialism," the huge influence other countries on local fashion, food — you name it. There was an enormous backlash against singer/dancer Carmen Miranda (perhaps most famous for her elaborate, fruit-encrusted turbans) when she made a successful career move to Hollywood in the 1940s. Many Brazilians felt betrayed, believing that Miranda didn't represent authentic samba, that she carved out an international career by playing up to Latin stereotypes, and that, in any event, she should have stayed in her native Brazil. (Miranda was actually Portuguese by birth, but she moved to Rio de Janeiro as a child.)

Similarly, in 1964, when Antônio Carlos Jobim, one of Brazil's best-loved songwriters ("The Girl from Ipanema"), played New York's Carnegie Hall for the first time, the response in his homeland was largely negative. Jobim was accused of being elitist and of allowing American jazz to influence his delicate, syncopated *bossa nova*. (He recorded with Stan Getz and with Frank Sinatra.)

Having said all that, foreign culture (especially American) is alive and well nationwide. Television is the single largest disseminator, in the form of dubbed sitcoms and other foreign programs, with Hollywood and European movies running a close second. Every corner snack bar serves hamburgers and hot dogs, and American pop music is played on radio stations everywhere. Kids think it's cool to speak English, and adults are finding that skill more and more necessary for business advancement.

Attitudes Toward Other Cultures

The U.S. influence on Brazil in the 20th century has ranged from the "Walk softly and carry a big stick" policy of President Teddy Roosevelt, to the "good neighbor" strategies of the Cold War to the cultural influences just mentioned. Some Brazilians see their northern neighbor as a mighty power to be emulated, others loathe that power.

In general, Brazilians like and respect Europeans, whom they believe to be more "civilized" than New World dwellers. Though they make fun of British "punctuality," German "inflexibility" and French "volatility," they hold these and other European cultures somewhat in awe. The one exception is Portugal. Take any ethnic or culturally derogatory joke ("How many _____ does it take to screw in a lightbulb?"), insert "Portuguese" as the subject, and you'll have a Brazilian laughing.

Generally a mystical and curious group, Brazilians are interested in all things Oriental, from religions to medicine, and they're in awe of Japanese creativity and the quality of their goods. Many urban Brazilians have converted to Buddhism; still others practice Chinese medicine or follow macrobiotic diets.

National Identity & Pride

In the late 1960s, a group of musicians led by Caetano Veloso and Gilberto Gil spearheaded *tropicalismo* — a musical rebellion that mixed "psychedelic" sounds, native Brazilian styles, and lyrics that alluded to world politics and the likes of anthropologist Claude Lévi-Strauss — after British and American music had taken the country by storm. (Both Veloso and Gil were jailed for their music, which authorities considered anarchical, and then went into exile in London for several years.) Since the recent death of Antônio Carlos Jobim, Veloso has inherited the mantle of Brazil's premier songwriter, and he's also one of the finest poets writing in Portuguese.

Olodum, a Bahia-based Afro-Brazilian music group and cultural advocacy organization, is now world-famous thanks to their participation on Paul Simon's album, "Rhythm of the Saints." (Olodum takes its name from the Yoruba word for "God of Gods.")

In more rarefied circles, those asked to name a Brazilian composer will immediately say Heitor Villa Lobos, a classically trained cellist who created the beautiful Bachianas and other works that combine the "erudite" with Brazilian folk tunes. For inspiration, he claimed to have studied his native country "city to city, state to state [and] forest to forest, scrutinizing the soul of the land [and] the character of the people."

Jorge Amado, the great novelist of Brazilian life, has had his work translated into over 40 languages. Many of his books were made into motion pictures, including *Gabriela* and *Doña Flor and Her Two Husbands*. Sultry actress Sonia Braga, who starred in Amado's above-mentioned films, has made a name for herself abroad with roles in *Kiss of the Spider Woman*, *The Milagro Beanfield War*, *Moon Over Parador* and *The Burning Season*, about the murder of Chico Mendes. (For more on Mendes, see Chapter 13: Business Outside the Law.)

Post-impressionist Candido Portinari — whose *War and Peace* fresco decorates the lobby of the United Nations' building in New York, while his *Discovery and Colonization* fresco is on display at Washington, D.C.'s Library of Congress — is possibly Brazil's best-known painter. Popular "primitive" artists, whose childlike oil paintings depict weddings, cane-cutters or angels, include Rodolfo Tamanini, Waldomiro de Deus and Ivonaldo.

In the sports world, the Santos Soccer Club produced the incomparable Pelé, who retired to become a sort of roving goodwill ambassador for his country. Brazil's national team won the 1994 World Cup for the fourth time, with very little government or corporate sponsorship — just a lot of hard work coupled with enthusiasm. The auto racing world still mourns Airton Senna, who died at the age of 34 in a May 1994 car crash during the Italian Grand Prix. Senna was second only to Alain Prost in his record of Formula 1 wins.

3   Cultural Stereotypes

Corrupt

Brazil is the land of impunity.

Brazil is a huge country with an inequitable distribution of wealth, and it's true that many are out to get all that they can for themselves alone.

This state of affairs has given rise to the expression *jeitinho* (literally, little way). Brazilians say that if you have a little *jeitinho*, you can get anything done. *Jeitinho* comes in handy when, for example, you've gone over your allowable limit on computer components or other luxury items abroad and now you must try to get them through customs. It may be in the form of a bribe or just by knowing the right person. (This is not to suggest that all or most customs officials are bribable.) But success stories are told by triumphant Brazilians returning from Miami, their baggage loaded with purchases that far exceeded standard regulations.

Jeitinho is also a way of bridging the gap between a very rigid bureaucracy and the natural informality of the people. A very useful social service is provided by the *despachante* (expediter), a paid professional who, through contacts and money, makes sure that your papers are on the top of the pile when applying for an ID card or any of the numerous other documents Brazilians are required to carry. This is a perfectly legal set of circumstances.

A cousin of *jeitinho* is the expression *"Você sabe com quem está falando?"* (Do you know who you're talking to?). It's common for many Brazilians to try to use what little power most of them have in a huge, bureaucracy-ridden country to gain a little advantage for themselves. When challenged by authority, when waiting in line for something, or when talking with a haughty maitre d', they'll often intone that lofty question and then proceed to inform their interlocutor of their important connections.

What's a Clock?

Brazilians aren't serious about time or commitments.

Brazilians tend to have a relaxed attitude about appointments and schedules. If a Brazilian is having a good time at the beach, he may just forget he's an hour late to meet friends for lunch. Because Brazilians are spontaneous, fun-loving people, they can appear to be somewhat frivolous to outsiders. An apocryphal tale has Charles de Gaulle remarking after a 1960s visit, "Brazil isn't a serious country." Many Brazilians take a smug pride in that. After all, they say, God is Brazilian, the country is beautiful, and the weather is nearly always amenable, so why worry?

A chat over a leisurely *cafezinho* (espresso) is a favorite way of socializing, and of doing business, for that matter. In seaside towns, the beach is the great common denominator, with the weather described only in terms of if it's a good beach day or not. In other words: *Carpe diem*, live for today. With all the uncertainties in life, Brazilians say, it's better to enjoy what you have right now.

Soccer & Sambas

All Brazilians care about are sports and music.

Four-time World Cup champions, the Brazilian national team plays as if it was born knowing how to kick. In fact, most Brazilian boys grow up kicking around soccer balls on the streets, with matches held every weekend in any available field or vacant lot.

The sport's rise to popularity among the poor is partly due to the fact that no equipment is needed other than the ball. Anthropologist Roberto da Matta points out that in Brazil's inequitable society, soccer represents a unique meritocratic niche — a player is judged on the basis of his talent alone, and even a kid from the slums can "make it big." (For more on soccer, see Chapter 19: Socializing.)

It's hard to find a tone-deaf Brazilian, or one who has no understanding of rhythm. It's not unusual to be sitting at a beachside bar on a Sunday afternoon and see a group of people suddenly start improvising, whether they know each other or not. Somebody will bring his guitar, and even the least musically talented of the bunch can tap out a rhythm on a box of kitchen matches.

Machismo & Violence

Brazilian men are brutal sexists.

For centuries, Brazilian courts looked the other way if a man killed his wife "in defense of honor" — in other words, if he caught her with another man. Such impunity still prevails in more remote areas.

Brazilian government sources estimate that 70 percent of the violence and abuse against its female population is committed in the home. In the bigger cities, police stations and shelters that specialize in handling domestic violence have sprung up, roughly 150 of them nationwide, but the demand far outweighs the help available.

Still, the feeling persists that one shouldn't interfere in what goes on between a husband and wife. Many men have mistresses, and many women are left home alone to raise their children. When their soccer team loses, some men get drunk and beat their spouses. It's also true that while some Brazilian women complain of being treated like sex objects, Rio de Janeiro is home to a booming plastic surgery industry that caters to many females who are willing to go to great lengths to attract and please.

The translation of machismo into large-scale violence is a fairly new phenomenon here. It began with the 1964 coup, when members of the military behaved as they wished with impunity. As has been the case with other Latin American dictatorships, many political dissidents "disappeared," though it's generally believed that incidents of torture and murder never escalated to the degree witnessed in Argentina and Chile.

Today, state police forces continue to be criticized for perpetrating human rights abuses, ranging from the ill-treatment of detainees to participation in death squads. In 1993, antiviolence programs were launched at the federal and state levels. According to government statistics, in the state of Rio de Janeiro alone, 131 members of death squads were indicted between 1993 and 1995, 64 of whom are in prison. Low salaries exacerbate the problem. Rio policemen receive promotions and significant pay raises for "bravery," which often encourages the "execution," rather than the arrest, of suspects.

Still, lack of education — about basic childcare, about job skills — is the biggest cause of fatalities nationwide. "Ignorance and its ills," writes *The Economist*, "kill more Brazilians in a month than violence does in a year."

Promiscuous

Sex is for sale everywhere you look.

Possibly by virtue of their tropical and subtropical climate, Brazilians are very comfortable with their bodies, and they're apt to be quite direct when flirting or making an advance. The poet Vinicius de Moraes, known best for his lyrics to Antônio Carlos Jobim's songs, wrote at the close of his 1939 "Sonnet to Fidelity:" *Que (o amor) seja infinito enquanto dure* (May love be infinite as long as it lasts). Still, the Catholic Church retains a strong moral influence. Whether Brazilians are actually more promiscuous than people in other countries depends on which survey you read.

During Carnival, the days of dancing and drinking that precede Lent, there's a lot of "fooling around." It's true that the country ranks high in reported AIDS cases. Foreign men are approached incessantly at the beach, in bars and in hotels by prostitutes or girls just looking for a good time at someone's expense. In some of the poorer coastal towns of Brazil, teenage girls offer themselves in the hope of one day being "taken away from all this."

Motels that rent by the hour are a staple nationwide, partly because most single Brazilians live with their parents and have nowhere to go for intimacy. In fact, the word *motel* means just that, a place to have sex, not a place to spend the night on a long car trip. (A word of caution: Visitors wishing to book lodging in Brazil should make sure they're reserving rooms in a *hotel*.)

A downscale version of the motel is the *drive-in* — called just that, in English. A *drive-in* is a parking lot in which the spaces are covered, separated by walls, and entered by drawing back a curtain, which is then closed for privacy. *Drive-ins* charge by the hour. Bar service is available.

A Nation of Street Children

Brazil is overrun with homeless children who run wild, succumbing to crime, drugs and prostitution.

Illegitimate children — often the progeny of Portuguese men and African or Indian women — have been a fact of fact in Brazil since colonization. They were usually absorbed by rural families and well taken care of. Today, however, these children often roam the streets, brutalized by society and often brutal themselves. Their number has been estimated at between eight and ten million.

Many aren't abandoned but "work the street," selling candy or washing windshields, often bringing home more money than their parents, who work as domestics or day laborers — minimum-wage jobs. However, others are regarded as a threat by merchants, who've been known to hire security guards or others to kill them. The childrens' plight came to worldwide attention in 1993, after eight such children were murdered execution-style as they slept, on a Rio de Janeiro street. Off-duty policemen were later convicted of the crime.

The Brazilian government, the Catholic Church, and international human rights groups all have programs in place to help get these kids off the streets and to educate and train them. Unfortunately, these programs fall short of meeting the needs of so many.

Regional Differences

Brazil is customarily divided into five regions, each with its own personality and culture.

The Southeast

Most businesspeople are likely to concentrate their efforts on the southeast, which includes São Paulo, Rio de Janeiro and Minas Gerais. Most of Brazil's service companies and industry, and much of its farmland, are located in these three states.

In São Paulo, less than 10 percent of the country's population produces more than one-third of the total gross domestic product. São Paulo is the world's third-largest city, and some estimate that it may hit the number one slot by the year 2000. It's also Brazil's financial center (Avenida Paulista is the city's Madison Avenue and the old downtown area is its Wall Street); the world's biggest producer of frozen concentrated orange juice; Brazil's biggest automobile and auto parts producer; and one of the country's biggest producers of footwear, appliances and chemicals. Its Santos Port is the largest in the world, in terms of frontage — though due to inefficiency and a surplus of red tape, loading a container here can cost double what it would in New York's harbor.

São Paulo boasts the largest Japanese community in the world outside of Japan — Liberdade — with a population of almost one million. And in nearby Americana — settled by Americans who fled the post–Civil War southern states — there's an annual picnic complete with young women in hoop skirts and their beaux in rebel grey uniforms dancing the Virginia reel.

Rio de Janeiro is a huge petrochemical and offshore crude oil producer. Many of the government-owned companies, including the oil monopoly Petrobras, are headquartered there. Rio's main industry, though, is tourism, both domestic and foreign. *Cariocas*, as the locals are called, are seen as a fun-loving bunch, ready to break into a samba at any moment.

Minas Gerais is a huge producer of metals, minerals, coffee, automobiles and steel products in general. The Mineiros are seen as hard-working, skeptical sorts "who've got to see it to believe it."

Businesspeople in this region are savvy and sophisticated. Most speak English and many have been educated abroad.

The South

The southern states of Paraná, Santa Catarina and Rio Grande do Sul are major farming areas. Paraná boasts the country's second largest port, called Paranaguá.

Santa Catarina was settled by Germans, and in cities like Blumenau, German is taught in the schools and Oktoberfest is celebrated, complete with bratwurst, lederhosen and musicians imported from Munich.

Natives of Rio Grande do Sul are called *gaúchos*, and many of them dress similarly to the Argentine *gaúchos*, with leather chaps and cowboy gear. Other inhabitants are of Spanish or Italian descent, and most speak a second language, usually English.

The Center-West

Bordering Bolivia, this region is home to the capital city, Brasília. Much of it is savannalike terrain, with huge farms and cattle ranches extending as far as the eye can see.

The states of Mato Grosso and Mato Grosso do Sul boast a beautiful wetlands area called the Pantanal, where toucans and parrots fly overhead and fish and alligators abound. The Pantanal covers 88,803 square miles (230,000 km) and is Brazil's second-most-important biological reserve after the Amazon. Large patches of it become submerged during the rainy season.

Most folks here live the cowboy life. Indeed, horses are the main means of transportation for many. Center-West Brazilians are tough, good-hearted and appreciate the wide open spaces and "big sky" landscape.

The Northeast

Brazil was discovered by the Portuguese near Olinda, in the northeastern state of Pernambuco. It is thus the oldest developed region in the country. Neighboring Bahia is said to be the heart and soul of Brazil: its mixture of African and European people has given rise to some of the country's most highly prized food, dance and music. The *berimbau* (a bowed, one-string instrument) comes from here, as does the *cuíca* and other percussion instruments.

The northeast and the north are the nation's poorest regions. Inequitable income distribution, resulting from centuries of feudal-like economic practices, has left many areas in the region as poor as some African countries.

Although Brazil's lengthy coastline is dotted with gorgeous beaches from north to south, most Brazilians prefer the beaches of the northeast. Northeasterners are known for their musicality and a laid-back life-style that natives of other regions sometimes laugh at — but most secretly envy.

The North

Much of this region is occupied by what's left of the Amazon rain forest — although routine slash-and-burn farming is threatening to do away with the delicate ecosystem altogether. The government has strict rules about land use here, but due to the region's sheer size and the corruptibility of poorly paid inspectors, they're hard to enforce.

Until recently, the government itself was guilty of rainforest devastation. Two huge mining projects — Carajás and Serra Pelada — wreaked destruction, much of it irrevocable, on both plant and animal life.

Carajás, an 18-billion-ton iron ore mine in the southeastern Amazon, consumed billions of dollars, borrowed mostly from foreign governments and the World Bank in the 1980s. It's an example of Brazil's scramble to alleviate its foreign debt by mining and exporting ore.

The Serra Pelada gold mine, discovered in 1980 in the same region, was immortalized by photographer Sebastião Salgado, whose blunt black-and-white shots of miners trudging up and down the walls of the huge pit with bags on their backs was reminiscent of a giant anthill. The pit has since mostly run dry, with any residual mining now mechanized. Unfortunately, the mercury used to separate gold from sediment still courses through the rivers.

Despite this escalating and seemingly doomed scenario, the Amazon rain forest still contains the largest single reserve of organisms in the world — estimated at between 800,000 and 5 million species, or 15 to 30 percent of all the species in the world. As naturalists catalogue new species of freshwater fish, their findings suggest that there may be as many as 3,000 different kinds in the region's rivers and lakes, including *pirarucu* (the largest freshwater fish in the world), *tambaqui* (with teeth so strong they can crack hard rubber tree seeds) and the dreaded *piranha*.

The North is both extremely poor and very remote. You can travel hundreds of miles before encountering any sign of human life here. The main arteries are the rivers. Very few railroad lines exist, and the Trans-Amazonian Highway has long been overgrown by the jungle. (Malaria pills and yellow fever shots are recommended for both the north and northeast regions. A hepatitis vaccination is also a good idea.)

5. Government & Business

Curbing Inflation ... Finally

For nearly four decades, hyperinflation reigned in Brazil. At one time in 1989, the currency fell at a rate of 80 percent a month; in early 1994, the annual rate had spiralled up to an incredible 7,000 percent. Then, on July 1, 1994, the government introduced a stabilization plan that included a new currency, the *real* (plural *reais)*. The effect was immediate. Inflation dropped to 18 percent in the second half of 1994 and has gradually decreased since. Inflation in 1997 is expected to come in under two digits.

The government then began a broad effort to further stabilize the economy through sweeping market-oriented reform, including public sector and fiscal reform, privatization, deregulation, and the elimination of barriers to foreign investors. These efforts are now bearing fruit. In 1995, private businesses — including Volkswagen AG and Brahma SA (who is erecting Latin America's largest brewery) — invested some US$1.8 billion in the economy. However, there's is a lot of fine-tuning going on. Restrictions abound on credit, for both consumers and institutions, and trade unions are still under the aegis of the Labor Ministry.

While Brazil is open to foreign trade, it's also deeply concerned about the balance-of-trade deficit that its new "open" policies have engendered. From time to time the Central Bank or the Commerce Ministry will impose or alter import financing regulations or non-tariff trade barriers. (The Central Bank, far from being an independent institution like the U.S. Federal Reserve Board, is beholden to the Ministry of Finance.)

Brazil has institutionalized the role of *despachante*, a sort of private expediter between business and government. These expediters make it their business to know all the right people. They're familiar with the various government departments and their required paperwork, permits and licenses.

Mercosur

Brazil is a founding member of the South American trading bloc Mercosur, established with Argentina, Paraguay and Uruguay in 1995, with Chile and Bolivia joining in 1996. Joint tariff exemptions and the gradual aligning of financial markets are two aims of this common market. Another is to form a united front through which to negotiate with such counterparts as the European Union and the North American Free Trade Agreement (NAFTA) — thereby lowering or eliminating import duties on products traded between member nations. Their ultimate goal is to extend membership to all South American countries before linking up with NAFTA by the year 2005.

Barriers to Trade and Competition

Brazil imposes quotas on automobile imports with a twofold purpose: to narrow the trade deficit

Government & Business

by limiting the outflow of hard currency, and to protect the local industry. Aside from these quotas and import duties on high-end consumer goods, Brazil has enthusiastically opened up its economy to trade. The country was an ardent participant in the General Agreement on Tariffs and Trade talks that bought about the World Trade Organization, and it has a permanent delegation to that group.

Brazil restricts some imports to protect local industry. At the same time, it's importing capital goods to modernize its industrial base and become more competitive. Brazil has a sugar export quota, to reserve enough raw material to produce the ethanol that fuels half the country's naval fleet. Also, much like OPEC members, it restricts coffee exports in accordance with quotas set by the London-based Association of Coffee Producing Countries.

According to the U.S. Department of Commerce, areas where trade barriers still exist include,

- **Services.** Under Brazil's 1988 Constitution, foreign financial institutions are restricted from entering the country or expanding pre-1988 operations. The Brazilian Congress approved five constitutional amendments in 1995 that eliminated the distinction between national and foreign capital; opened the state telecommunications, petroleum and natural gas distribution monopolies to private (including foreign) participation; and permitted foreign participation in coastal and inland shipping. However, the degree to which these sectors are actually opened will depend on implementing legislation. Legislation permitting the licensing of private cellular phone networks to compete with existing parastatal monopolies was passed in 1996, but it requires majority (51 percent) Brazilian ownership of eligible companies.

- **Investments.** Various prohibitions restrict foreign investment in petroleum production and refining, internal transportation, public utilities, media, shipping, and other "strategic industries." In other sectors, Brazil limits foreign equity participation, imposes local content requirements, and links incentives to export performance. Also, new restrictions were introduced in the auto sector. Foreign ownership of land in rural areas and adjacent to international borders is prohibited.
- **Computer Technology.** The 1991 Informatics Law stopped requirements for government prior review for informatics (computer technology) imports, investment, or manufacturing by foreign firms in Brazil. However, import duties remain high (up to 35 percent) on computer products, and Brazilian firms receive preferential treatment in government procurement and have access to certain fiscal and tax benefits. For a foreign-owned firm to gain access to most of these incentives, it must commit to invest in local research and development and meet export and local training requirements.

  The Software Law of 1987 requires that all software be "catalogued" by the Informatics Secretariat of the Ministry of Science and Technology prior to its commercialization in Brazil and that software to be run on Brazilian-origin hardware be distributed by a Brazilian firm. However, a draft law has been introduced into Brazil's Congress to eliminate these two requirements.

Privatization

Privatization (which allows foreign investment in companies the government is divesting) has been heralded as the single most important transition from a closed, Third World country to a major player on the international marketplace. Between 1991 and 1997, Brazil sold off 55 companies for a total of US$15 billion. Though privatization isn't moving along as quickly or as smoothly as some would like, it's understood that attracting foreign capital and foreign technology is essential if Brazil is to modernize its infrastructure and finance its growing trade deficit.

Critics point out that the legislation needed to create the regulatory framework for the privatization process was put on hold for nearly two years while Congress wrangled with the issue of a second presidential term. Brazil's 1988, post-military regime Constitution limited the president (as well as governors and mayors) to a single term. After much back and forth between factions and the upper and lower houses, Congress finally voted in June, 1997, to allow a president a second, four-year term.

But when the model for comparison is Chile, for example, it's easy to see why Brazil's process is taking longer. The city of São Paulo alone is the size of Chile and its GDP is greater, points out Luiz Forbes, the New York–based international representative for the São Paulo Stock Exchange (*Bolsa de Valores de São Paulo)* and Commodities and Futures Exchange (B*olsa de Mercadorias e Futuros*). "Chile," he explains, "has done a magnificent job privatizing its social security system, but, in all due respect, it is a smaller, more manageable economy."

Some former government monopolies, such as the petrochemical and steel sectors, have been successfully privatized, with both national and foreign capital participating in the different consortia created to buy the companies. The *Companhia Vale do Rio Doce*, the world's largest iron ore producer, recently sold off 41 percent of its assets to a private group (which includes a U.S. bank) led by the *Com-*

panhia Nacional de Siderurgia (the National Steel Company, itself recently privatized).

In some cases, foreigners are being allowed to purchase minority stakes. This will force many to find local buyers, and such joint ventures will almost certainly change the country's rather insular business world. Brazil's phone companies (both the holding company Telebrás and the individual state phone companies) will probably be privatized by the turn of the century. Banks, electric and natural gas utilities, shipping services, and Rio's subway system are also on the privatization list.

Again, the Constitution, which mandates the government monopoly on petroleum, needed to be amended before the sector could be open to competition. "Changing a constitution takes time if you live in a democratic country," adds Forbes, who was formerly president of the Brazilian-American Chamber of Commerce.

However, the national oil company *Petrobrás* has stubbornly resisted all sales attempts, with strong popular support. Created in 1954, the national oil company's slogan is *O Petróleo é Nosso* (The oil belongs to us) and that mind-set continues today. In the past, *Petrobrás* held the monopoly on oil exploration, prospecting and distribution. Under the new law, that monopoly shifted to the federal government, effectively empowering the administration to open drilling and refining to the private sector. But such a decision is very probably years away.

The Stock Market

Stock trading is preponderantly concentrated in São Paulo, although Rio de Janeiro and other cities have their own exchanges.

Initial public offerings are a rarity, though gung-ho market enthusiasts hope to see that change in the next few years. Right now, the market is dominated by the state-owned companies that trade some of their shares. *Telebrás*, the holding company for Brazil's 27 state phone companies, is often responsible for 50 percent of all stock trades on any given day. The other big players are *Eletrobrás*, the power utilities holding company, and *Petrobrás*, the oil corporation.

Decades of high inflation made fixed-income investments, whose ever-higher returns were indexed to the spiraling inflation rate — a much more attractive option than the stock market. But now, with inflation at a low and steady rate, the market has become attractive again, with most of its stocks still greatly undervalued.

However, the São Paulo Stock Exchange suffers from a vicious circle of illiquidity. Investors prefer the New York Stock Exchange (NYSE) or one of the other big exchanges, where they can be assured of an adequate number of buyers and sellers. São Paulo trades about US $700 million on an average day, compared with US$20 billion on the NYSE.

The same holds true for the São Paulo futures exchange. It's the fourth biggest commodities exchange in the world (after Chicago's two markets and the exchange in New York), but most of its volume is in interest rate and foreign currency futures, not commodities. Again, producers prefer to hedge their crops on one of the big exchanges because they're more liquid.

The Work Environment

Status in the Workplace

Hierarchy has a strong (though not always apparent) role. While merit-based promotions are common, it certainly helps to be ingratiating with your boss. Especially in the more old-fashioned, family-run operations, it's good policy to let the boss think he's making all the decisions, even when it's the staff who come up with the final recommendations.

There's a close-knit "old-boy" network that functions both nationwide and regionally. Many top Brazilian executives are Masons, for example. On a regional basis, the elite belong to the same clubs and eat at the same restaurants. Their wives go to the same hairdressers and shop at the same boutiques. Senior executives and managers will occasionally socialize with their underlings at a Christmas party or to celebrate some profitable deal, but generally, each stratum pretty much keeps to itself.

Racism: Unspoken But Evident

Race remains a sensitive and largely unspoken issue. Although most Brazilians will hotly deny the existence of any racism in their country, the office environment, from manager level up, is basically a white male's world. Few blacks or women are seen in top executive posts (or, for that matter, in top academic or governmental positions). According to the United Nations, income inequality in Brazil is the most extreme in all of Latin America. Speaking with a *Wall Street Journal* reporter, Justice Ministry official Ivair Augusto dos Santos admitted that "The companies that discriminate the most in Brazil [against non-whites] are Brazilian companies. The best are the multinationals...." Levi-Strauss & Co. has made racial diversity an explicit hiring goal, and it funds an antidiscrimination education group. Monsanto Company even runs an internship and a scholarship program for black students. "When mutltinationals *do* discriminate," dos Santos continued, "it's usually because the directors are Brazilian."

There's talk in government circles of *acão afirmativa* (affirmative action) and of establishing quotas, both for business hirings and for higher education opportunities. (Though blacks and mixed-race people make up 45 percent of the population, the University of São Paulo, the nation's largest public university, is 99 percent white.) In 1996, President Fernando Henrique Cardoso established a commission, headed by a black man, to draft compensatory policies that targeted Afro-Brazilians.

Still, many oppose, or deny the need for, mandated equality. Others see it as an administrative nightmare. In such a multiracial land, how would categories be determined? And with corruption and cronyism common in government circles, how could an affirmative action program be kept on track?

Brazil's Constitution forbids discrimination on the basis of race or gender. Ironically, though this is often largely ignored when blacks are the victims, it may be that quotas favoring them will be found unconstitutional. However, one sign of hope is that in early 1997, São Paulo elected its first black mayor.

Seniority

The process of seniority differs, depending on the type of business — family-owned, government-controlled, or others.

In family-owned businesses (and some of the biggest companies in Brazil are still run by families), primogeniture prevails. Eldest sons take over the reins of the companies from their fathers. In their absence, control goes to a daughter or nephew.

Look at the masthead of most major newspapers and you'll see that board members share a last name. This is not to say the newspapers aren't objective. The Brazilian press is, on the whole, highly respected internationally, and most publications hire professionals from outside to run day-to-day operations on both the editorial and the sales sides.

Seniority at government-controlled companies, while subject to corruption, is usually on a merit basis. Employees at many of these companies must take continuing education courses and tests in order to advance.

It is probably the big-city financial institutions that have the most equitable seniority policy (and the highest quality top managers). Many banks, for example, hold periodic "career-day" testing for job applicants. These tests are advertised in the newspaper and the results are often made public. Once you're "in," your promotions are based on a combination of education, performance and tenure.

Levels of Education

School is compulsory and free for seven-to fourteen-year-olds in Brazil. However, the quality of that education varies greatly, and in poor areas (notably the northeastern countryside), many children drop out early, either to help their families earn money or because parents believe that the available schooling is worthless. In 1991, the country's overall illiteracy rate for those over the age of 15 was 20 percent.

So while most of the finest universities offer free tuition, public school students rarely qualify for enrollment. Aspiring college students must go to private school and then, in many cases, take a year-long, private preparatory course to get them through the tough college admissions exam.

Most office workers will have had a high school education augmented by some extra courses in, for example, secretarial skills or accounting. From middle-management up, Brazilians tend to have educations rivaling those of their U.S., European and Asian colleagues. Indeed many have earned their MBAs abroad. However, they can get an equally good business education at home. The private Rio de Janeiro–based Getulio Vargas Foundation, with a branch in São Paulo, is one of the top-ranking business schools in the world. It's also a fine research institute that supplies the government with much of its economic data.

Until the 1980s, multinationals sent executives from the home office to run their Brazilian operations. Now, the Brazilian executive class has come of age. One example eloquently illustrates the level at which Brazilian executives now find themselves. The Bank of Boston recently appointed Henrique Meirelles, formerly president of its Brazilian branch, as head of its Boston-based worldwide operations.

The Problem with Pensions

Brazil is something of a paradise for pensioners — at least for some. For a start, there's no minimum retirement age. Some retired people (a.k.a. inactive workers) draw more than one pension — one former *estado* governor enjoys five, legally — and some receive both a pension and a wage. Others receive a higher income in retirement than they did when they were employed, and their pension increases whenever their working colleagues get a wage hike. According to *The Economist*, "some tailors, having never left Brazilian soil during the Second World War, but having sewed the uniforms of an expeditionary force that did, are still drawing generous war pensions" as of 1997. And the civil service pays out about six times as much in pensions and insurance benefits as they receive in contributions. Politicians, the most privileged group, need work only eight years before qualifying to retire on full pay.

These schemes, combined with controlled inflation and an aging population, are contributing greatly to Brazil's overall economic woes. Reforms are slow in coming. However, for the vast majority of the population, a pension amounts to less than a minimum salary.

Women in Business

Traditional Roles

With the exception of the largest cities, the prevailing attitude toward women is that their sole destiny is as wives and mothers. Outside of actresses and models, few Brazilian women have made a name for themselves. One exception was Maria Bonita, the wife of an outlaw named Lampião. Together with Lampião's gang of bandits, they roamed the *sertão* (an arid, savannalike region in the northeast) in the 1930s, eventually meeting their death in a shoot-out with the federal police. Today, Maria and her husband are the subject of folk songs and stories; they're seen as heroes who represented a kind of freedom many Brazilians long for.

Another exception is Clarice Lispector, a Ukranian immigrant, who is considered one of Latin America's foremost women writers. Lispector writes in an arch yet mysterious style about society's ills. Her short story, "A Hora da Estrela" (The Hour of the Star), was made into a film in 1985.

Until quite recently it was unheard of for a woman to live alone. Even today, most women live with their parents until they marry. However, it should be noted that many men in the more traditional regions do likewise.

Women and men have equal rights in marriage, and they can wed under one of two systems: community property or separate property. With the former, community property is split equally after a divorce; under the latter, each spouse recovers whatever pre-existing wealth was brought to the household. Still, in the event of a break-up, men usually end up paying alimony and women usually get child custody.

Voting and Other Rights

In 1932, a short twelve years after the 19th amendment was passed in the U.S., Brazil became one of the first of the Latin American countries to grant national women's suffrage. In comparison, Brazilian women enjoyed voting rights years before their counterparts in France (1944), Japan (1945) and Switzerland (1971) did.

With suffrage came an awareness of other women's issues, such as just compensation, regulated work weeks, safe working conditions and maternity leave. Until the late 1970s, however, additional opportunities (as well as participation in the Brazilian feminist movement) were limited almost entirely to educated, middle- and upper-class women. Since then, a newly democratic Brazil has opened doors for working-class women into decision-making organizations and political groups.

Today, roughly 40 percent of the female population aged ten years or older work outside their homes, according to government statistics. A growing number of them are pursuing professional careers. Half of the students presently enrolled in colleges and universities are women.

The 1988 Constitution contains several provisions that consolidated women's rights dating back as far as the early 1930s. Coincidentally, it was in 1988 that Luiza Erundina de Souza — an unmarried woman from the impoverished northeast region and a Marxist to boot — broke all precedents by winning São Paulo's mayoral race. And in 1995, Brazil's Congress received its first black female senator. The Constitution also established a woman's right to take 120 days (18 weeks) of paid maternity leave, and it guaranteed that she would be given an equivalent position upon her return to the workplace. Sexual discrimination or bias in the workplace, including discrimination in hiring and compensation, is now illegal, although, like laws against racial discrimination, it's very difficult to monitor.

Strategies for Foreign Businesswomen

Women negotiators should be aware that they may encounter difficulties dealing with Brazilian male counterparts. One African-American woman, sent to Brazil by her New York-based company to set up a partnership with a local distribution network, heard this question again and again: "So, when is your boss coming?" When she finally — politely and firmly — established that she was the boss, the negotiations sailed to a successful conclusion. In fact, she was constantly entertained during her visit with dinners and trips to the beach. Once she proved herself to be a professional, the barriers were eliminated.

Another thing women need to keep in mind is that sexual harassment, unless it's blatant to the point of rape, isn't seen as an issue here. When a man compliments a woman, he's usually just behaving as custom dictates. Complimenting a woman is considered polite. That doesn't mean there won't be cases when a man will try to exceed the bounds of the professional relationship. It's true that many Brazilian men will consider you fair game because of your gender. Common sense and discernment should prevail.

8. Making Connections

Cultivating Relationships

Many foreigners tend to see Latin America as a single entity. But having a business in Mexico, El Salvador or Uruguay, for example, won't necessarily help you establish connections any more easily than having a business based in Miami.

Cold calling is one way to make initial contacts; having a written or oral introduction isn't necessary. Lists of Brazilian companies abound — at embassies and consulates worldwide, chambers of commerce, or on the Internet. Large international consulting companies like Price Waterhouse or Arthur Andersen have "Brazil desks" to help you get started.

Regarding Telephones

Brazilians aren't the world's promptest businesspeople when it comes to returning phone calls. Don't be afraid of calling again and again, day after day or even several times a day, if the business at hand is urgent. A Brazilian's sense of time and urgency is probably different from yours.

Get your counterpart's cell phone and pager

numbers. Find out who his most important assistant is and get that person's numbers, too. Don't assume that just because you've sent a fax, it was received. And remember, the Brazilian telecommunications system is woefully obsolete. It's up to you to keep the ball rolling.

There are approximately nine lines per one hundred people, and one in four calls may not get through. According to *The Economist,* some ten million people are currently waiting for a line, and those who are in a hurry must pay somewhere between US$2500 and US$7500 for the privilege of getting one sooner. The government has promised to install 35 million new lines, including cellular connections, by the year 2000.

9

Strategies for Success

Relationships Before Business

The importance of establishing good personal relationships in business can't be overemphasized. And once they've been established, maintain frequent contact on both business and social levels. Most Brazilians are outgoing and friendly, and they prefer to work with people they know and trust.

Offer your Brazilian counterpart details of your life; show him photographs of your children, talk about your favorite sports (a little praise for the Brazilian national soccer team will be warmly received), tell him a story of something funny that happened to you on your trip.

Brazilians like to talk about their lives and will ask what some might view as very personal questions. One mildly overweight woman executive was fawned over by the receptionists who greeted her upon her arrival at a Brazilian manufacturer. They wanted to know when her baby was due. Having been prepared for such questions, she took no offense. Instead she laughed with them about their mistake, and proceeded to show them pictures of her "children" — two poodles and a cat.

Eight Keys to Business Success

1. Never underestimate a Brazilian's education, knowledge or intelligence. Always talk to your counterpart as an equal. The culture may be different from yours, but any Brazilian in a managerial position probably has as good an education as you do. If a Brazilian perceives that he's being patronized, you may as well consider the deal terminated.

2. As previously noted, Latin America isn't a single country. Always keep in mind that Brazil is larger than the contiguous U.S., that it has a completely different culture from its Spanish neighbors, and that it features distinct regional differences.

Brazilians consider themselves to be Americans. Therefore, avoid the phrase "in America" when referring to the U.S.

3. Never address a Brazilian in Spanish. Even if your gesture is well-meaning, it will be taken as an insult. Brazil's native language is Portuguese."It's as if I walked into a business meeting in New York and started off by saying 'Guten Tag,'" one Brazilian consultant explained. "It shows total disregard for the country, its history and its people."

4. It's not necessary to know Portuguese, although a few key terms (especially the all-purpose *tudo bem*) will be appreciated. Brazilians have a sense of humor about the foibles of learning another language (many have studied some English in school), and they appreciate any attempt made by foreigners to communicate in Portuguese. Businesspeople will either speak English or provide an interpreter, very likely one of their secretaries. Many universities offer degrees in becoming a "bilingual secretary" — a profession that's recognized by the government and roughly equivalent to an administrative assistant.

5. Be aware that your Brazilian counterpart is likely to know more about finance than you do, as

he's spent years grappling with astonishingly high inflation and interest rates. He'll be able to quote fixed-income returns, tally up accrued interest in his head, and give you the exact inflation rate for December of 1992. In fact, most taxi drivers can do the same. Such knowledge, a weapon against hyperinflation, was a matter of survival for so long that it's become ingrained.

6. If you bring a gift to your first meeting, make sure that it's something unique, something your contact couldn't get elsewhere — perhaps a coffee-table book published for your company for private distribution. Whereas twenty years ago it set a good tone to bring a bottle of Scotch (which could sell for as much as $200 in Brazil), today such a gesture will be considered offensive. When in doubt, don't bring anything. (For more on gift giving, see Chapter 16: Customs.)

7. Try not to change your negotiating team midstream. Brazilians will want to take the same amount of time they took to acquaint themselves with you to get to know the new members. This will inevitably delay an agreement.

8. In some cases, you might find it advantageous to talk over a business breakfast or drinks (perhaps at your hotel's bar), and always at your invitation. It's not only a good way to get to know your counterpart in a stress-free environment, but it also sets an informal tone that will carry over into more detailed negotiations in more formal settings.

10

Time

Deadlines & Appointments

Be aware that Brazilians use a 24-hour clock, so 5 P.M. becomes 1700 hours. Also be advised that for most Brazilians, the notion of time is somewhat arbitrary. This isn't a nation of clockwatchers.

Expect Brazilians to be late for meetings, and expect them to disregard deadlines. By adopting this approach (painful as it may be for you), you'll be delighted when someone does show up on time. By no means is tardiness a sign of disrespect on a Brazilian's part; indeed, it reflects a perception of time as a flow of events, rather than as a segmented pie of minutes and hours. They believe that what someone is doing right now may be so important that the next item simply has to wait. You, of course, will always be punctual. It's expected.

Traffic is often evoked as a cause for lateness. Be aware that traffic is, in fact, terrible in the big cities. Rain causes rivers to swell and flood the roads, causing back-ups of several miles.

If a deadline is crucial, it's best to inform all of the parties involved of that fact. Do so tactfully, and preferably in writing. Set up progressive steps that can be checked along the way to ensure that the deadline will be met, and be sure you check those steps as things progress.

11 Business Meetings

Arranging the Meeting

A meeting can be arranged between your secretary and your counterpart's secretary or directly between two executives. Most educated Brazilians speak English or have, at the very least, studied it to some extent in school.

If you intend to hold several meetings during your stay, or to visit several companies, don't arrange your schedule too tightly. The odds are that during the course of a week-long trip, with visits planned to, say, five different companies, not everything will proceed as planned. Airline pilots may go on strike without notice, meetings can be cancelled for no apparent reason, roads may wash out...

A loose schedule will also allow you some free time for an impromptu meal or excursion with the people you're going to meet. You may find that such spontaneous events turn out to be the most profitable "meetings" of your entire visit.

Preparing the Brazilians for the Meeting

Anything you can send along in advance — company history, an outline of your proposal, and so forth — will be appreciated. If you can send materials in Portuguese, so much the better. Attach a nice pen or business-card holder decorated with your company logo to the materials you send.

Don't expect to spend too much "quality time" on the telephone with Brazilians prior to the meeting. They want to see your face, and things agreed upon (other than time and place) by phone may not be acknowledged later, when the face-to-face meeting takes place.

Arriving at the Company

Brazilians often extend the courtesy of having their visiting foreign counterparts met at the airport and taken either directly to the company or to their hotel. Private chauffeurs are much more common in Brazil than in most other countries. It's a nice gesture to tip the driver, who probably makes little more than minimum wage.

Telling Who's Who

Upon your arrival at a company, you will generally be met by a receptionist, who will take you to a meeting room or to your counterpart's office. You may also be met by his assistant, who'll "break the ice" as you await the boss's arrival. Remember, the meeting isn't likely to start on time, so use this opportunity to acquaint yourself with the surroundings.

It's perfectly all right to make discreet inquiries as to the hierarchy. It's unlikely that you'll be able to discern it by the uniform dress or appearance of a group of mostly white males. If you can ask your interpreter quietly, so much the better. The oldest person in the group is probably the most senior, but this isn't always the case — especially in Brazilian financial institutions, where U.S.-trained whiz kids are gaining more and more status.

Presenting Your Business

You and your counterpart(s) will exchange business cards at the beginning of the meeting. Brazilians will often bend over a top corner of a card, in a gesture that "personalizes" its presentation.

At first, the conversation will be informal. You'll start off by talking about other topics. Your counterpart will almost certainly ask if you would like a *cafezinho*, a glass of water and/or fresh juice, and inquire about your trip.

Brazilians are simultaneously emotional and shrewd. In the course of sizing you up, they'll observe not only the quality of your shoes, let's say, but also how *simpático* (nice, amenable) you seem.

Once the initial niceties have taken place, maybe after 10 or 15 minutes, you can start presenting your business — in a straightforward, pleasant manner. If you're using handouts, be aware that in Brazil, periods are used to denote thousands and commas denote fractions, so that $1,000.00 is written $1.000,00. The medium is the message, so use good quality presentation materials and audio-visuals.

Direct your comments to the whole group but particularly to the highest-ranking individual and decision maker. Answer questions openly, don't appear defensive, and never "talk down" to anyone in the room.

It's likely that the final decision won't be made by one person alone. The decision-making structure is multileveled, and it could be that the people you're negotiating with aren't the ones responsible for the final decision — especially if it's one of those huge family-owned companies. They'll kick your proposal upstairs, as it were. However, their input will be seriously considered.

Concluding the Meeting

If you (wisely) arranged your meeting for 10 A.M. or 3 P.M., you might find that at its conclusion, everyone will go out to lunch or drinks or dinner together. If you're invited along, it's a good sign. Whatever you do, don't demand a decision on your proposal immediately. Give the group time (hours, days or weeks, depending on the situation) to consider and discuss it among themselves.

12. Negotiating with Brazilians

Environment and Tone

Negotiations may require a little more time than they would in G-7 countries (those with the world's highest GDPs). Foreign businesspeople eager to cut a deal in Brazil are often frustrated by how long things take to accomplish.

Do your homework, and be very clear about what you plan to present. It helps if you've learned everything you can about the Brazilian company in advance.

Listen carefully to your counterpart, and don't attempt to second-guess him. Remember, Brazilians deeply resent being patronized and you can lose a battle instantly if you seem to be questioning someone's intelligence or background. Debating the facts is, of course, another story. But do so in a respectful, equal-to-equal way. **This can't be emphasized too strongly.** Also, humor is greatly appreciated and if you can keep the stress level down, you're likely to score more points.

Be prepared for the possibility of having to negotiate with more than one group. Logistics might have to be addressed to the technical department, while budget issues will be presented to the financial department.

Some decisions may not rest solely with the company. Government bureaucracy could step in. That's why it's so important for you, or more likely, the Brazilian company, to have that all-important *despachante* (expediter) on hand to help figure out if something is do-able, and if it is, how to do it in the most efficient manner

Above all, be patient. And remember: Brasília wasn't built in a day.

Interpreters

There are universities and universities, and not all bilingual secretaries who've earned their degrees are equally skilled.

If your counterpart offers you a secretary or an assistant to interpret, try speaking with that person on the telephone first. If you're not comfortable with the person's fluency, there are other sources available for translators and interpreters. In Brazil, it's big business. Berlitz is a widely recognized supplier; in São Paulo and Rio de Janeiro, there are professional associations that can put you in contact with one of their members. Again, a chamber of commerce or a Brazilian mission abroad is your best bet for access to these services.

They don't come cheap. Expect to pay around $200 a day for a good interpreter, with a $100, four-hour minimum. If you need *simultaneous* interpretation, as during a lecture or presentation, expect that fee to double.

Tips on Using Interpreters

1. **Establish Guidelines**

   Before a meeting, plan with your interpreter the mechanics of how you'll work together. For example, how long you should speak before pausing for interpretation? Ideally, you should practice extensively with your interpreter even before your trip. Go over any specialized vocabulary, brief him (or her) thoroughly in advance of negotiations, and provide him with as much written material as possible. Also, give him time to become familiar with your style, humor, and body language, so that he can accurately convey your messages.

2. **Don't Exhaust Your Interpreter**

   During a meeting or negotiating session, stop every couple of sentences to allow for interpretation, and try to limit each sentence to one main point. Don't begin another sentence before the interpreter has finished translating the previous one. Interpreters need to rest at least every two hours. If negotiations continue for more than a day, you may need two interpreters. Prepare to be patient, as using an interpreter can stretch a meeting to three times its normal length.

3. **Address Your Brazilian Counterpart**

   When using an interpreter, look toward the head of the Brazilian team, not at the interpreter. Brazilians value personal communication and may understand more English than they let on. Speak slowly and clearly, and avoid idiomatic expressions and slang.

4. **Review What's Been Said — Anticipate What's Coming**

   During breaks, review with your interpreter the main points that both sides have made. Ask your interpreter what he observed or noticed about the other side's position or behavior. Try to get a feel for the direction in which negotiations are headed, and anticipate what will need to be said later on. This will help your interpreter to present your case in the most favorable way possible.

5. Emphasize Important Points As They Arise

Abstract or complicated discussions are seldom directly translatable. An experienced and qualified interpreter will tailor his translations to reflect your style, level of formality, tone, and intended meaning. You can help ensure that important points get across by repeating or emphasizing them and by making certain that your verbal and nonverbal (body language) messages are consistent with each other.

The Brazilian Approach to Contracts

Brazilians view contracts as binding agreements. However, they tend to like long words, lots of adjectives and flowery speech. The Portuguese translation of an English-language contract will be about 20 percent longer than the original. And be aware that Brazilians use periods to punctuate thousands and commas to delineate fractions.

Hire the services of a local accountant, lawyer, or *notário* (similar to a lawyer) to help with contract issues. Many Brazilian law firms have branches abroad that specialize in drawing up international contracts. Some specialize — in intellectual property rights or informatics legislation, for example. Engaging one of these firms is a wise investment.

13. Business Outside the Law

Underground Economy

The underground economy is thriving and Brazil's byzantine tax system allegedly encourages it. Critics claim that taxes are high and that they see very little benefit from them. Indeed, much of Brazil's tax revenue is earmarked for payroll: the government, its agencies and companies are bloated to the point of bursting, despite frequent attempts at administrative reform.

The barter system is common. Masons exchange services with dentists and teenagers baby-sit in return for English lessons. Street vendors are everywhere, some licensed, others, not. Everyone, from the guy at the airport exit to the hotel concierge, will offer to exchange currency for you. Taxi drivers will try to strike a deal without turning on the meter.

Drug Gangs and Numbers Rackets

Illegal drug trafficking is big business. In fact, it drives much of the crime in places like Rio de Janeiro. While not as huge or as wealthy as Colombia's cartels, Brazil's drug gangs are quite powerful.

Business Outside the Law

Gang leaders learned their organizational skills from political prisoners with whom they shared jail cells during the 1960s. Today, these men are seen as de facto mayors of their respective *favelas*, as they contribute a percentage of their proceeds to their communities.

Partially processed cocaine is brought over the border from Bolivia or Colombia and refined in the Brazilian outback, where materials are more easily available than in the source countries. It's then trucked to the Atlantic seaboard and smuggled onto planes and ships. Visitors returning home from Brazil are likely to encounter drug-sniffing dogs at their port of entry. (A note of caution: Brazil's drug laws are extremely tough, and foreign embassies aren't in a position to be of much use if a visitor is arrested.)

Until the early 1990s, a group of rich and powerful men known as *bicheiros* (bankers) ran the country's illegal numbers racket. Their success was credited to two factors: cunning and sponsorship — of the *escolas de samba* and the annual Carnaval *samba* parade, as well as of amateur soccer teams, — especially before corporate sponsorship became available. Most of the famous *bicheiros* have since been apprehended and are living out their days in white-collar prisons.

"Living contraband" is another lucrative, illegal endeavor. Most prized are woolly spider monkeys, fewer than 400 of which are believed to exist in the world; they sell for up to US$50,000. Also in demand are hyacinth macaws. With fewer than 3000 in existence, they fetch between US$15,000 and US$20,000 apiece. It's even illegal to have a parrot as a house pet, though many do.

Graft & Corruption

According to a 1996 poll among international executives, conducted by Berlin-based Transparency International, Brazil was cited as one of the 15 most corrupt nations in the world. And that corruption is self-perpetuating (despite recent government crackdowns), spawned in huge government-owned monopolies and bloated federal agencies, then filtered down to the general populace.

An entire generation of Brazilians, in their 30s, have only recently begun to develop a political consciousness. Their parents' generation, living under military rule, had no say in their country's decision-making process.

The country's first directly elected president, Fernando Collor de Mello, is an example of how entrenched corruption is at the upper levels. He resigned in December, 1992, after two years in office, rather than face corruption charges in a Senate impeachment trial. He now lives "the good life" in Miami.

Such centralization has led to immense disparities in Brazilian society. The current democratically elected administration is trying to deal with corruption, at least at the federal level. Nepotism, long a favorite way of taking care of friends and family, has now been outlawed. The government is trimming its payroll and has begun to privatize some of its huge industries and utilities. The Treasury is cracking down on tax evaders, and corruption trials are being expedited more swiftly than in the past.

Present Changes and Future Outlook

Brazilians are starting to feel more a part of the political process and a sense of community spirit is starting to grow. But Brazil's democracy can be

Business Outside the Law

compared to a child with severe growing pains. After centuries of tight, centralized rule in which the country was divided into the "haves" and the "have-nots," ironing out the vast social inequities is going to take another decade or two, at best.

Huge landowners — especially in the poorer and largely illiterate regions of the Northeast — continue to call the shots and influence the vote among people unaccustomed to voting. That influence has sometimes extended to murder — the most well-known example being the 1988 assassination of Chico Mendes, a community leader whose fight for the rights of fellow rubber tappers in the Amazon exploded into a worldwide environmental crusade, a crusade at odds with the landowners' plans for rain forest exploitation.

Bribery remains common. (One foreign citizen said that her company paid US$5,000 to anonymous bureaucrats in order to expedite her residence visa.) Members of Congress continue to enjoy huge salaries and such perks as free plane tickets to their electoral districts, free housing, and generous expense accounts. Though prostitution and gambling are illegal, both are rampant.

If the government continues on its current tack of prioritizing education and social welfare, it's likely that some past wrongs will be righted. Private enterprise is making a valuable contribution to Brazilian society by sponsoring schools, day-care centers and training programs.

14. Names & Greetings

Order of Names

Brazilians almost always go by their first names. Employees of Mr. Marcelo Vieira will call him *Senhor* Marcelo, not *Senhor* Vieira. For women, *Dona* is used much more than *Senhora*, so if a female boss or an older woman is named, say, Eliana Davila, she would be addressed as *Dona* Eliana (regardless of her marital status).

The first-name tradition is so prevalent that telephone books in small towns alphabetize subscribers by their first names (suggesting a sense of community that's nearly nonexistent in the larger cities). So many Brazilians share common last names (such as Silva or Souza) that they're often better known by their first names or nicknames.

Although Brazilian Portuguese has two forms for "you," as do most European languages — the second person *tu* and the third-person *você* — the *tu* form is more of a regional distinction than one suggesting intimacy. Most Brazilians use *você* in all circumstances. There's yet another, even more formal, form of address: *o senhor* and *a senhora*. While this form is considered extremely polite, one that a Brazilian would use with strangers and older people, foreigners aren't expected to master it.

Titles, Business and Otherwise

While Brazilians are informal in conversation, they do like titles. Practically anyone with a college degree of any kind is referred to as *Doutor* or *Doutora*. It's also a formality used by cab drivers, waiters and other members of the service industry when addressing customers.

In corporate circles, a company's chief executive is usually called the *Presidente*. *Diretor superintendente* is equivalent to a managing director or vice president of a division. Next down in the hierarchy is the *Diretor*, then the *Gerente* (manager).

VERY GOOD   **I DON'T KNOW**   **FULL OF PEOPLE**

15. Communication Styles

Body Language

Don't be surprised if, walking down the sidewalk parallel to a busy street, you see two people on opposite sides of the street making plans to meet later in the day for a drink at a designated bar — without uttering a single word. Brazilian body language and hand gestures are so refined that they not only enhance spoken language, they sometimes even replace it.

Gestures have different meanings in different countries. Two that are considered obscene in Brazil are:

- Slapping the fist into the palm. It has a sexual connotation, though in locker room situations, it can mean a macho "Go get 'em."
- The circled thumb and forefinger, associated in many parts of the world with "OK," means "asshole" here. If you want to indicate "OK," use the "thumbs-up" gesture.

Some Popular Brazilian Gestures

- Pulling at the earlobe indicates that something — a wine, a piece of music — is very good.
- Drawing your thumb and forefinger against your mouth has a similar meaning, usually with regard to food.
- Tapping a thumb quickly against one's finger tips means "full of people," as when describing a bus or a concert.
- From the *favela* gangs: Pretending to polish your nails on your chest means "Watch out" or "Danger."
- Quickly shaking your wrist, causing the fore finger to slap against the middle finger, means "Hurry up" or "Go for it!"
- A shrug means "I don't know," a nod indicates "yes," and shaking one's head stands for "no."

Guidelines

1. Everyone shakes hands, even children. When you arrive somewhere, and when you depart, you're expected to shake hands with all present.

2. Greetings can include everything from embraces to a series of kisses (two or three) on alternating cheeks. It's normal for someone to lay their hand on your arm to make a point.

3. Brazilians stand closer to one other when speaking than many Westerners are used to. Refrain from backing away.

16 Customs

Carnaval

Some historians trace the carnival tradition back to Ancient Greek festivities. During the Middle Ages, it became a feast that preceded Easter and the forty-day Lenten season, during which pleasures of the flesh were put aside. It came to Brazil via the Portuguese, who celebrated it with practical jokes and informal street dancing, and evolved into a slick, sophisticated, week-long celebration of the senses.

Today, *Carnaval* is the country's single most important holiday. Everything grinds to a halt as the *escolas de samba* parade down the streets of cities and towns nationwide — from sunset until long past sunrise. Dances are held at clubs and ballrooms. The dress code? The citizenry dons masks, sequins, feathers, paint, and the briefest of costumes, and it's not unusual for women to remove their tops as the evening progresses.

Carnaval is a way of forgetting the mundane world which, for many, has little to recommend it. It celebrates the absurd, the grotesque and the erotic (men don huge fake breasts or penises and offer them to passersby, singing *Mamãe, eu quiero mamar,* "Mama, I want to suck milk"). And it represents defiance against the country's sometimes repressive history. Anthropologist Nancy Scheper-Hughes puts it this way, "*Carnaval* is both the opiate (or the metaphorical speed or crack cocaine) of the popular classes *and* their symbolic Molotov cocktails. *Carnaval* crowds are unpredictable; they can explode and turn from revelry to protest."

Brazil's biggest and glitziest *Carnaval* parade is held in Rio de Janeiro. Foreigners wanting to attend should get tickets through a package from their travel agent; tickets in Brazil sell out swiftly.

Locals often spend the entire week at the beach; wealthier Brazilians who dislike all the hubbub escape to their country retreats. (These are the summer months in Brazil, and many families go on extended vacations.) Don't attempt to schedule any business activities during this time, and be aware that a lot of business slows down during the entire period between Christmas and *Carnaval*.

Samba

Historians believe that *samba* derives from *semba*, a word common to many West African Bantu languages. However, whether *semba* means a cry, a complaint or something like "the blues," or whether it refers to a fertility rite that involves the violent bouncing together of navels, is open to debate. As with American blues and gospel, its roots are ascribed to plantation work songs.

The first known appearance of *samba* as a Portuguese word meaning a rhythm and a dance was in the newspaper *O Carapuceiro* in 1838. In 1917, Ernesto dos Santos recorded what's now viewed as the first official *samba* song — "*Pelo Telefone*" (On the Telephone).

Samba speaks of a sadness so overwhelming, so inclusive of everything from homesickness to lost dreams to man's essential solitude that, in the end, it can only be celebratory. In *Why Is This Country Dancing?*, author John Krich quotes an elderly Brazilian on the importance of *samba* this way: "Without *samba*, there's an emptiness that can never be filled. It's the pill for our sickness, a medicine for the heart."

Gift giving

Brazilians are great gift-givers — at Christmas, on birthdays, often for no reason at all. If a person is celebrating a birthday, it's not at all unusual for him to invite a group of friends out for dinner and pick up the tab, not the other way around. But the friends will bring presents to the dinner or party.

If invited to a Brazilian's home for dinner, it's appropriate to bring flowers or wine. If you get to know your Brazilian contact well, on a second or third trip you might bring the person something you know he or she is interested in or that's unavailable in Brazil. A book, a specialty food item, or perhaps a video (all Brazilian VCRs are adapted to the U.S. system) will be appreciated.

17. Dress & Appearance

In the big cities, corporate people dress as corporate people do most everywhere — in business suits. Women have a bit more latitude; they'll wear casual dresses and go bare-legged in the summer. Despite the heat, shorts are taboo, except at the beach. Both genders tend to follow European styling, though American clothing fads are popular with teenagers. Shoes should be kept in good repair. Brazil is an important footwear exporter, and people tend to take shoes very seriously.

Dress is more casual for social occasions, although there are still a few restaurants in São Paulo that demand that men wear coats and ties. Women tend to dress up more than men do in the evening. You'll often see the man in a couple in shirt sleeves while the woman is in a cocktail dress and pearls. Tuxedos and floor-length gowns are rare.

In general, women's clothing tends to be revealing and tight-fitting. And bathing suits for both sexes are usually microscopically small. The thong bikini (called *fio dental* — dental floss) was a Brazilian invention.

In smaller towns, in the hot northern region or on farms, people are much more casual. Ties are practically unheard of, and many people wear shorts. Air conditioning isn't always available in remoter areas.

Ethnic Attire

Many ethnic groups don special costumes to celebrate "old country" holidays or feasts. German and Austrian enclaves in the south hold Oktoberfest gatherings, while the Chinese community in São Paulo rings in Chinese New Year in grand style. Afro-Brazilians nationwide, led by the Olodum music group and other organizations, celebrate African feast days with music and dance.

18 Entertaining

Restaurant Etiquette

Lunch is usually the biggest meal of the day. Brazilians sit down to dinner as late as 8 or 9 P.M., and it's not unheard-of for the meal to last until the early hours of the morning. (If you're dining with business counterparts, reserve any business topics for after the meal.) All cities have a wide variety of fine Brazilian, international, and other ethnic restaurants. Restaurants charge a 10 percent gratuity, which is included in the total bill. However, it's good form, although not required, to leave another 5 or 10 percent for good service.

Brazilians tend to eat everything with a knife and fork, including pizza, fruit and most sandwiches. In some cities, such as São Paulo, restaurant smoking is restricted. However, in most areas, smoking is quite common. If you choose to sit outside at a beachside restaurant in Rio de Janeiro or Salvador, for example, be prepared to deal with panhandlers and street kids. If they approach you, it's probably best to let your Brazilian counterparts deal with them.

The national drink is *caipirinha*. Made of fermented sugar cane juice (similar to rum), limes and sugar, it's a potent mixture. Refreshing *batidas*, made of the same liquor and shaken with any of a variety of fruit juices — similar to daiquiris — are also quite popular.

Turf and Surf

Brazilians are avid carnivores. They love steak and pork loin. Be prepared for a phenomenon known as *rodizio*, a system in which waiters bring skewer after skewer of grilled meats — ranging from chicken wings to huge hunks of steak — to your table and slice bits off onto your plate. At most *rodizio* restaurants, small wooden cubes painted green on one side and red on the other will be placed next to each plate. As long as the green side is up, the waiter will keep coming back.

Feijoada is a pork lover's delight. It contains various parts of the pig, including ears, snout, feet and sausage, simmered with black beans and spices. While its ingredients may sound a little unappetizing, the final product is a tribute to the ingenuity of slaves who were tossed the less desirable remains from the masters' Sunday dinners. Traditional side dishes are rice, steamed kale and orange slices, this latter thought to "cut the fat."

At family-style restaurants, *feijoada* is served bubbling hot in an earthenware bowl. At more expensive restaurants and hotels, *feijoada* is set up buffet style, allowing the discerning adventurer to pick and choose which meats he wants.

With a coastline that stretches from the warm equatorial waters to the frigid South Atlantic Ocean, Brazil offers fish and seafood galore.

Along with the above, each region has its own specialties. Of particular note are the foods of

Bahia, which are heavily influenced by African cuisine. Seafood stews flavored with okra, coconut milk and *oleo de dendê* (a particularly pungent form of palm oil) are usually quite spicy and beg for cold beer to wash them down. *Acarajé* is a deep-fried bean batter mixed with shrimp and spices, x*inxim de galinha* is chicken in peanut sauce, and *quindim* is coconut pudding.

The south of Brazil is known for its excellent wines. Generations of Italian and German immigrants have taken advantage of the rolling hills and temperate climate to produce both reds and whites of high quality.

Churrascos

Brazilians who live in the country, have second homes there, or have homes at the beach love to invite hordes of friends and family over on weekend afternoons for a *churrasco* (barbecue). Visitors who are invited to one of these afternoons of hedonistic pleasure should consider themselves lucky, and they should expect to be the focus of many questions. Your hosts will want to know what you think of this, did you enjoy that, is this strange to you, had you ever heard of that before?

The hosts (and their servants) take care of everything; guests aren't expected to do anything except have fun. There will be the ubiquitous *caipirinhas* and music, along with an ongoing game of volleyball, frisbee or bocce for entertainment. If there is an important soccer game being televised, some people might retire to the house to watch it.

19 Socializing

Beach Culture

Praia (the beach) is Brazil's great equalizer, a democracy unto itself, where everyone goes to swim, take the sun, and play. Beach volleyball is popular, as are other sports on the sand. Beaches tend to be crowded year-round.

The beaches are set up as little communities. Urbanized beaches offer showers, sanitary facilities, dune buggies and food stands. Entertainment is provided by both professional and amateur musicians. Unspoiled beaches, especially in the north, offer long stretches of pristine sand dunes and palm trees.

Near almost every food stand, a group of people will set up at one of the picnic tables and while away the afternoon drinking beer and playing music. Most Brazilians would rather play their own music than listen to it on the radio. In the bigger cities, particularly Rio de Janeiro, the beaches are well-policed by multilingual officers in uniforms consisting of shorts and T-shirts.

Soccer = A Religion

Brazil has elevated soccer to an art form, and the game provides a source of national unity. It's taken extremely seriously, and World Cup losses, notably the one to Uruguay in 1950, are said to have caused more than one suicide.

Every four years, during the World Cup, business grinds to a halt as everyone watches the Brazil games — either in their offices, at home, or on big outdoor screens. When Brazil gets to the semifinals, businesses send their employees home. The employees work extra hours after the series to compensate for the time off. Fights break out during matches, but Brazilian fans are no more violent at games than many of their European counterparts.

Even those unfamiliar with the sport will note a difference between Brazil's style and that of any other national team. Brazilian soccer players seem almost to be dancing. Indeed, this dance is echoed by fans in the stands, who beat out samba rhythms and other traditional chants during matches.

Bars & Music

The *barzinho* (little bar) is the gathering place for groups of friends, both in the city and in the country. *Barzinhos* are inexpensive and very simply adorned, and customers can just as easily stand at the bar for a quick coffee as spend the afternoon at one of the rickety tables, watching a soccer match on TV or, again, singing songs. In smaller towns, some bars are frequented only by men.

When a Brazilian doesn't have any other plans, he'll end up at the *barzinho*, discussing the day's news and having a drink with the friends he's bound to run into there. It's a home away from home, especially for those who live in cramped city apartments. Customers develop informal credit relationships with the barkeepers, often settling up at the end of each month.

Padarias (literally, bakeries), are similar gathering places. Some people go there for their morning *pãozinho* (little bread) and coffee, while others hang out at them, especially the ones that have TV sets and serve beer. These establishments are also open on Sundays.

Gambling

Though gambling was outlawed in the 1940s, it's alive and well. It's most popular manifestation is *jogo do bicho* (literally, animal game) in which players bet on animals representing sequences of numbers. The game runs twice daily, and bets can be made on street corners or in local bars. The payoffs are small but frequent, with the average daily bettor winning something at least once a week.

TV Globo

The world's fourth largest television network in terms of advertising revenue, TV Globo rivals the Catholic Church as the largest single influence on the populace. Its broadcasts reach virtually every town in the country, and it has often obtained viewer ratings of 100 percent. None of the other Brazilian networks runs even a close second.

Some small towns in the northeast have no electricity — but each has a television set propped up on an outdoor platform in the center square, powered by its own generator, invariably tuned to TV Globo. The keeper of the keys unlocks the protective case around the TV set in the afternoon and then locks it up again after the late news, around midnight.

Owned by the Marinho family of Rio de Janeiro

(they also own a vast media conglomerate of newspapers and radio stations), the Globo network has a conservative bent and has no qualms about openly supporting one or another political candidate.

Telenovelas: Life Imitates Art

But Globo's most stunning success is its slick, primetime *telenovelas*. They have a huge influence on Brazilian behavior and consumerism and have been exported to more than 100 countries. They can run six nights a week for eight months or longer, and unlike American "soap operas" (which are interminable), they have endings. If it's an especially big hit, there will be hardly a soul on the street. Everyone watches them, from janitors to corporate lawyers. People meet for dinner *after* the *telenovela* broadcast.

Telenovelas have such a grip on the Brazilian viewing public that when Daniela Perez, a hugely popular young star of *De Corpo e Alma* (With Body and Soul), was found murdered — stabbed eighteen times with a pair of scissors — three days after Christmas in 1992, the announcement of President Fernando Collor de Mello's resignation went largely unnoticed. The young man convicted of killing her, Guilherme de Pádua, was one of her *telenovelas* co-stars. Just hours prior to Perez's death, the two had filmed an episode in which Pádua played the angry boyfriend she'd just broken up with. (Both Perez and Pádua were married, and Pádua's wife was pregnant at the time.) According to testimony at his trial, Pádua had taken his role so much to heart that he'd been unable to differentiate between real life and the script — which, in an added irony, had been written by Perez's mother.

20. Basic Brazilian Portuguese

English	Portuguese
Yes No	*Sim* *Não*
Good morning/Good day Good afternoon Good evening/Good night Good-bye	*Bom dia* *Boa tarde* *Boa noite* *Tchau*
Please	*Por favor*
Thank you	*Obrigado (for men)* *Obrigada (for women)*
You're welcome	*De nada*
I'm sorry	*Desculpe*
My name is_____	*Meu nome é ____*
I don't understand	*Não entendo*
Do you speak English?	*Fala* inglês?

21 Correspondence

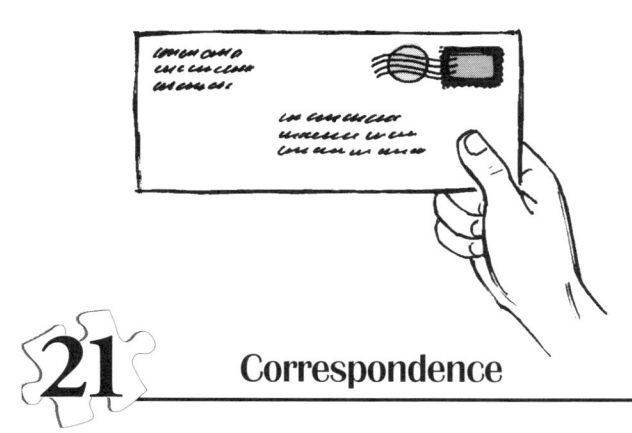

A Brazilian address is written as follows:

Sr. (or Sra., for a woman) Edson Arantes
Avenida Paulistano, 33, Sala 456
12345 São Paulo
BRAZIL

Note that the street number comes *after* the street name. Sala means room or suite.

You can begin the letter with *Caro* (dear) *Edson*. Brazilians rarely go by their last names. The customary closing is *Atenciosamente* (with deference).

Such honorifics such as *Ilustríssimo* or *Excelentíssimo* are still in use, especially within the government and old-fashioned companies, but foreigners aren't expected to use them.

22. Useful Telephone Numbers

These are local numbers. When dialing from outside Brazil, dial your country's international access code, then Brazil's country code [55], then the city code without the zero.

City codes

Rio de Janeiro	(021)
São Paulo	(011)
Brasília	(061)

Police	190
Ambulance	192
Fire	193
Road accidents	199
Tourist police (Rio)	(021) 511-5112
Local operator	100
Domestic long-distance operator	101
Local directory assistance	102
Operator-assisted collect call from a pay phone	107
International operator	000111
Avis	(011) 543-1333 / 535-4722
Hertz	(011) 214-8900; (021) 221-9708
Varig Airlines (São Paulo)	(011) 534-0122
Rio de Janeiro	(021) 220-3821
Brasilia	(061) 242-4111

23. Books & Internet Addresses

The Brazilians, by Joseph A. Page. Addison Wesley, Reading, Massachusetts, USA, 1995. An engaging and well-researched look at what makes Brazil so Brazilian, using examples like the phenomena known as "soccer madness" and the pervasive influence of *telenovelas*.

In the Cities and Jungles of Brazil, by Paul Rambali. Henry Holt and Company, New York, USA, 1993. This young journalist's portrayal of Brazil, based on stays spanning a half-dozen years, brings a stark, realistic touch to the travel writing genre.

The Politics of Military Rule in Brazil, by Thomas Skidmore. Oxford University Press, New York, USA, 1988. A well-documented account of one of the darkest periods in Brazilian history by a respected scholar.

The Masters and the Slaves (Casa Grande e Senzala), by Gilberto Freyre. Translated by S. Putnam. Alfred A. Knopf, New York, USA, 1964. Brazil's leading anthropologist addresses the origins of Brazilian culture in this landmark book.

A History of Brazil, by E. Bradford Burns. Columbia University Press, New York, USA, 1993.

considered by many experts to be the best single-volume history of Brazil in English.

Travelers' Tales Brazil: True Stories of Life on the Road, edited by Annette Haddad and Scott Doggett. Traveler's Tales, Inc., San Francisco, California, USA, 1997. Engaging firsthand accounts of this diverse country.

Internet Addresses

Usenet group
soc.culture.brazil
Mirror site for Usenet's F.A.Q.'s
http://www.rede.com/vitoria/faqs/Brasil-faq.html
Gazeta Mercantil: Brazil's financial news daily
http://www.gazeta.com.br/
The Globe Trotter
http://www.livingabroad.com/globe/countries/braz.html
Brazilian Business Directory
http://www.brabiz.com/en/engmain.html
Links to business information
http://www.yahoo.com/Regional/Countries/Brazil/Business/Directories/
Brazilian Mission to the U.N.
http://www.undp.org/missions/brazil/indexfr.html
Brazilian Embassy in London
http://www.demon.co.uk/Itamaraty/welcome.html

Passport to the World Series
Your Pocket Guide to Business, Culture & Etiquette

Other Passport to the World Books

- Passport ARGENTINA • Passport BRAZIL
- Passport CHINA • Passport FRANCE
- Passport HONG KONG • Passport INDIA
- Passport INDONESIA • Passport ISRAEL
- Passport ITALY • Passport JAPAN • Passport KOREA
- Passport MALAYSIA • Passport MEXICO
- Passport PHILIPPINES • Passport RUSSIA
- Passport SINGAPORE • Passport SOUTH AFRICA
- Passport SPAIN • Passport TAIWAN
- Passport THAILAND • Passport UK
- Passport USA • Passport VIETNAM

Available from your local bookseller or order direct.

WORLD TRADE PRESS®
Professional Books for International Trade
1505 Fifth Avenue
San Rafael, California 94901 USA
Tel: (415) 454-9934, Fax: (415) 453-7980
E–mail: WorldPress@aol.com
http://www.worldtradepress.com
USA Order Line: (800) 833-8586

The Global Road Warrior

The *Global Road Warrior* is a compact worldwide reference resource for the traveling international entrepreneur.

It contains pragmatic travel and business information critical to daily survival while "on the road" internationally.

The *Global Road Warrior* is compact and tough enough to withstand the rigors of travel.

The top 100 countries of the world are covered. Each country listing includes:

Global Road Warrior
ISBN 1-885073-49-6
640 pages, 100 countries, charts, graphs, and maps

Travel Facts Visas and passports, immunization and emergency information are covered.

Communications Including how to use pay phones and use call back numbers to save on phone bills.

Business Services Need a translator? How about a courier, copy shop or printer? This section can help.

Technical Support Includes local support numbers for hardware and software vendors. Also electrical requirements, and vital information about how to access the Internet and check email.

Available from your local bookstore or order direct.

WORLD TRADE PRESS®
Professional Books for International Trade
1505 Fifth Avenue
San Rafael, California 94901 USA
Tel: (415) 454-9934, Fax: (415) 453-7980
E-mail: WorldPress@aol.com
http://www.worldtradepress.com
USA Order Line: (800) 833-8586